THE LAVENDER BUNNY

CATHERINE J MCAMMOND

The Lavender Bunny
Copyright © 2021 by Catherine J McAmmond

All rights reserved. No part of this publication may be reproduced, distributed, or transmitted in any form or by any means, including photocopying, recording, or other electronic or mechanical methods, without the prior written permission of the author, except in the case of brief quotations embodied in critical reviews and certain other non-commercial uses permitted by copyright law.

Tellwell Talent
www.tellwell.ca

ISBN
978-0-2288-3353-6 (Hardcover)
978-0-2288-3352-9 (Paperback)

My name is Kayla and I have a story to tell you. It started a while back when I adopted a wee bunny who I named "Floppy." What a dear fellow he was... with bright white fur and brown splotches. Floppy appeared one day in a pet shop near my house. I fell instantly in love with him.

When I brought him home, I tucked his cage in the corner of my room by my bed. It didn't take long for me to learn that bunnies like to stay up all night. He kept me awake with his bunny-like activities. Why? Well, he would scurry around playing and nibbling on snacks.

After a time, my mum (her name is Nicole) wasn't too sure about the adoption. She sneezed and had runny eyes whenever she was around Floppy.

But he was sooo cute! He welcomed me home every day with a scurry and a twitch of his pink nose.

But then something happened…

My brother, David, a two-year-old terror, discovered my furry friend.

One day, I left for school like I always do. My brother was still asleep. After downing some cereal, I made sure that Floppy had all the fresh water and food he needed. Then, I crept out the door to school.

When he woke up, David decided to venture into forbidden territory… my room. He peeked inside and spotted Floppy.

It got really messy after that. Imagine a can of lavender paint stored carefully under a board in my room. My mum likes to change the wall colours regularly so we have paint cans everywhere.

Minutes after David entered my room, my mum discovered him. She had panic written all over her face when she found Floppy drenched in lavender paint.

My brother didn't really understand what he did, but he knew he had crossed the line as he watched my mum feverishly cleaning Floppy's fur.

The next day, it was with great sadness that I sent an email to everyone I knew, pleading for someone to give Floppy a new home.

In my email, I wrote, "Free to a good home: Adorable lavender bunny called Floppy. I have to find a home for my pet bunny. My mum is allergic and I have a two-year-old brother. Contact Kayla for more info."

And then I waited...and waited... and waited.

There seemed to be a lack of interest in my offer. I had to think hard. I could not return Floppy to the pet shop. Who knows what could happen to him? Floppy could have been adopted by someone who is unkind to animals.

Then Grandma Ruby came to my mind. When I called her, she was determined to decline my offer to give her Floppy.

She said, "I don't want pets to look after. Bunnies make a mess. Don't even think about bringing over that bunny."

Grandma Ruby didn't have much life in her voice anymore. Her heart just didn't have the same hop.

After that, Mum and I decided to pay Grandma Ruby a visit. We took Floppy. If she would watch Floppy over the weekend, we assured her that we would return to pick him up. I had a ringette tournament to play in so he needed a bunny sitter.

Mum and I had smiles on our faces as we drove away.

At the end of the weekend, I called Grandma Ruby to say we couldn't make it over to pick up Floppy. There was a major snowstorm on the highway. Grandma was not amused.

The next day, I called again. There was a quiet pause on the phone. Grandma said, "Don't rush over to get Floppy. He is fine."

As it turned out, Floppy never did make it back to our home.

Why, Grandma Ruby is busy. She has bunny food to buy, a cage to tend to, and cuddling to do.

Bunny rules!!

Whenever we have a family gathering, we all have to listen to the details of Floppy's daily routine. I love it, but other family members seem to roll their eyes with boredom.

Grandma Ruby discovered that Floppy delights in games. He drags an old towel to her. As he clamps gleefully onto the towel, Grandma swirls him around. Being airborne gives him more joy.

There are games of escape and capture too. Floppy is growing and so is his living space.

After all, Floppy needs Grandma as much as Grandma needs Floppy. The hop is back in Grandma's heart!

Oh! Did I mention that Floppy's new name is "Baby"?

www.ingramcontent.com/pod-product-compliance
Lightning Source LLC
LaVergne TN
LVHW070047070526
838200LV00028B/418